Do You Know How to Shut Up?

and 51 other

L I F E ☑ L E S S O N S

that will make you uncomfortable

MICHAEL STAVER

Mac Daddy Publishing
28 South 10th St.
Fernandina Beach, FL 32034

Copyright © 2008 The Staver Group

ISBN-13: 978-0-9801857-0-6
ISBN-10: 0-9801857-0-X

Library of Congress Control Number: 2007909835

Published by:
Mac Daddy Publishing
28 South 10th St.
Fernandina Beach, FL 32034

TABLE OF CONTENTS

ACKNOWLEDGMENTS

The creation of this book has been amazing in many ways. The most amazing part is that it is actually complete and in your hands. I am thankful, first of all, to *you*. Few people in the world care enough about themselves to improve themselves. So, congratulations, and thank you for having the courage to pick up the book and at least read the acknowledgments.

I am profoundly grateful to my Mom and Stepdad on so many levels. Thanks for suggesting that I write about what ultimately became the title for this book. Maybe you can convince the people you told me about to read it.

To my brother Corey, thanks for your wisdom, insight, and willingness to push me to do what I need to do. The way you manage relationships is truly admirable and a great model to follow. Oh yeah, and thanks for all the lunches...oh wait, I buy! To my brother Rich, your intensity and willingness to work through challenges inspired several chapters. Most importantly, though, you are a great dad.

My deepest thanks to Maxx. Thank you for letting me learn to be a dad, sometimes at your expense. You are headed for greatness!! Work hard, play hard!! Now go clean your room.

My thanks also to everyone at DeHart & Company. Your persistence and intensity around this project made it what it is. You guys are great, and you make me look good, which is a feat beyond any miracle I know. Special thanks to you, Dottie. I wish Celia were here to see this.

Deborah Dunham, thank you for believing in the message and the messenger. This would never have happened without your diligence and commitment. Thank you for all you do. The Staver Group is better because of you.

To Bobbie Stanton and Mary Anne Rybak, the keepers of my schedule and life at the company, thanks for no middle seats and most importantly for understanding my craziness and pace. You

i

guys keep me straight, and clients all over the world appreciate that as much as I do.

Reggie Tyler, for years and years you have been saying the book is the thing. Well, here it is. Thanks for your patience and persistence and for being a great friend.

To my friends Pam and Donald Skipper, thanks for always standing by with encouragement and willingness to help, and for having the insight to tell me it's time for a vacation.

Tina Ammons, thank you for reading and rereading and for your creativity about getting this work out there. I appreciate you.

Finally, I would like to thank all the thousands of people I have been blessed to work with over the years. You have taught me what I convey in this book—yes, even those of you who really annoyed me, especially the lady on the plane from Atlanta to L.A. who had no clue how to shut up…for *five hours*!

INTRODUCTION

First of all, thanks for taking the time to read what you are about to read. Few things in life are more important than intellectual, spiritual, and emotional growth. That's what this book is about. Here is fair warning: *Do You Know How to Shut Up?* DOES NOT convey some tell-you-what-you-want-to-hear "happy talk" message. (Did the title clue you in?) It is a compilation of practical, no-nonsense suggestions and, in some cases, directives on the subjects I am most often asked about.

My book is intended to help you bridge the gap between what you say you want and what you actually get. Let's face it: most of us are really good at talking about what we want, and not so good (in fact, in some cases, pathetic) at being willing enough to actually do what is necessary to achieve our dreams. Follow the advice herein and you can change that reality. You can learn to live your life and work your work in a way that is centered on accomplishing results.

Read this book any way you want to. A little at a time, all in one sitting, front to back, back to front…it really doesn't matter as long as you read it. Certain chapters will resonate more strongly at different times of the year and at different points in your life, so keep the book close by and reference it from time to time.

I wrote this book slowly over a period of several years. But long before I put pen to paper (well, actually, fingers to keyboard), I *lived* this book. I am still living it, in fact. During the editing process, some of the chapters hit me harder now than they did when I wrote them. While following my own advice is sometimes difficult, I believe in every word and have seen the impact of their application.

Notice I didn't say the change process will always be fun. It won't. But once you make the effort to start living the life you really want to live, you'll be thankful this book came along to provide a much-needed kick in the pants. You're welcome.

~ Mike Staver

CHAPTER ONE

L I F E ☑ L E S S O N

Do You Know How to Shut Up?

Have you ever been in a conversation with someone who made her point but just had to add a few other comments before letting it go? Or listened to a speaker who said, "In closing" about five times before he actually closed? Annoying, isn't it? It's also counterproductive.

I was recently working with two people who were attempting to resolve a conflict. At least three times it appeared that the issue was resolved until one or both of them added a "parting shot." If you have kids, you experience this all the time. But adults are just as guilty. While some people don't even know *when* to shut up, I have found that the larger number just don't know *how* to shut up.

Some people are simply uncomfortable with silence. Others just lack the skills to wrap up a conversation/debate/speech. Still others are so convinced that what they have to say is so important that they must say it in 10 or 100 different ways. Learning how to shut up is a valuable skill in business and in life.

Remember, friends don't let friends talk themselves into a hole. Since I know none of you *ever* suffer from this problem, take a look at the steps so you can share them with your friends as a little communication hint.

Here's how to shut up:

1. Be clear with yourself about what you are attempting to communicate.

2. Share with the person (when it isn't obvious) what you want to accomplish.

3. Avoid, at all costs, getting distracted by other issues, ideas, points, stories, and so forth.

4. Use talk-ending techniques like:

    a. Saying "So, what are the next steps?"

    b. Using an example that sums things up (if it is a public presentation). (Then stop.)

    c. Focusing on getting to the end of what you have to say in minimal time.

5. Give information in an amount the listener can reasonably digest—not the amount you personally feel compelled to share.

6. Ask someone you know and trust to give you feedback on the degree to which you are clear and the degree to which you are concise. It is very important that you are both.

In closing (and don't worry, I'm going to say it only once!), stop talking. Tolerate silence. It won't kill you!

CHAPTER TWO

L I F E ✓ L E S S O N

Are You Burned Out?

There I was sitting in the Atlanta airport waiting for a flight when—WHAM!—I got hit with what felt like a bolt of lightning. Screaming kids, inadequate air conditioning, flight delay, and two weeks on the road all contributed to the realization that I simply was not happy. I didn't want to do this anymore. I was burned out. It would be a mistake to believe that this experience could be solved with sleep, food, more time at home, or a vacation. Trust me, I tried all those things and none of them worked. Here's why: There is no relationship between working too many hours and burnout. The issue is how much meaning you find in your life and work. That day at the airport, I came face-to-face with the reality that I was investing energy in activities that did not give me a high rate of satisfaction. This realization was an almost palpable shock to my system.

Burnout always happens because our investment of energy is increasing while the return on that investment is decreasing. Have you ever been doing something you love to do, then looked at your watch and realized two hours had passed when it felt like only two minutes? Or worse, have you ever done something you hate to do and found that two minutes felt like two hours? Continuing to invest energy when there is a decreasing rate of return physically, mentally, emotionally, or spiritually will always result in burnout. The only way to avoid that is to change your energy investment strategy.

In my case, I had allowed the demands of helping people to exceed my ability to manage those demands. So I chose to limit the scope of my investment of energy. I did some simple things. No travel on Sundays...a schedule that was under my control (instead of the control of others)...choosing to work with clients who respected my work and were aligned with my company's core values...a significant decrease in (and in some cases elimination of) time spent on personal relationships that were parasitic. All of these changes helped. But the greatest help was the realignment of my energy investment strategy with my core values. I had allowed myself to drift; now, I had to rein myself back in.

Here is how to avoid burnout or come back from it:

1. Acknowledge that you are burned out or are burning out, and that it is the result of the way you are investing energy and the choices that you are making. Don't blame it on anything other than that.

2. Don't quit investing energy. Change where and how it is invested.

3. Become clear about what kind of return/results you want.

4. Be clear about your values.

5. Share your commitment to change the way you invest energy with someone who can hold you accountable for those changes.

6. Align your choices and behaviors with that commitment.

   a. If talking to your _____ (insert "mother-in-law," "overbearing neighbor," "demanding ex-wife," or so forth), exhausts you, then limit those conversations.

   b. If the account you have been trying to get keeps giving you the runaround, try another strategy or try another account.

CHAPTER
THREE

L I F E L E S S O N

How Independent Are You?

We live in a country that celebrates independence, and that's a good thing. But it occurs to me that perhaps it's time to reflect on our own personal independence, or lack of it. "Growing up" requires moving from a dependent way of life to an independent one. We celebrate employees who can take initiative and work independently. It makes us proud (and scared) when our kids demonstrate independence and responsibility. But I think it is a good idea to think about the extent to which independence works...or doesn't.

Excessive *independence* is no healthier than excessive *dependence*. Striking a successful balance requires a focus on three things: areas that are uniquely *yours*, areas that are uniquely *theirs*, and areas that are shared. Personal or professional relationships can work only when these three areas are blended. For example, in a work setting there are areas of your work that are all yours and work better if you hold on to them yourself. There are other areas that you may be tempted to get involved in but shouldn't. Then there are areas in which multiple people should get involved.

In your personal life, the same applies—time that is uniquely and protectively yours, time that is uniquely theirs, and time that is shared. If it is your kids' burden to carry, let them carry it. If you carry it, you will create unhealthy dependence. Force yourself to balance the paradox of dependence with independence. Are you so independent that those around you do not feel needed or important in your life? Do the people at work know you'll do it or redo it, so why try in the first place? Do you celebrate being free from the burden of perfection?

Here are the steps to remember:

1. Be clear about those areas at home and at work that are uniquely yours.

2. Be clear about those areas at home and at work that are uniquely theirs.

3. Commit to maintaining your independence, while at the same time depending on others when appropriate (as opposed to only when it's comfortable).

4. Let go of your limiting beliefs (i.e., I need them to get this done, or the converse, I don't need anyone).

5. Check in with others to determine the extent to which you tend to sway one way or the other. Others can generally see you more clearly than you see yourself.

CHAPTER
FOUR

L I F E LESSON

Do You Speak
Your Truth?

In our professional and personal lives, most of the success we encounter is the direct result of speaking our truth. It's all about being completely honest with ourselves and with those around us. I have noticed that the times in my life when I have found myself in the best place is when I make a rigorous commitment to speaking my truth. Conversely, failing to honor that commitment has led to negative consequences. I'm sure you can relate.

Have you ever been in a situation in which you knew what you really needed to do or how you really needed to show up—but didn't? Felt bad, didn't it? Speaking your truth can be as simple as saying *no* to a friend because you really don't want to go out, or as complex as saying *yes* to a challenging job or new relationship that you know is right for you but that intimidates or scares you.

Here are the steps to speaking your truth:

1. Pause and really pay attention to what your gut tells you.

2. Focus on your own internal truth before speaking or acting. Sometimes that quiet truth, heard only by you, is much more powerful than what is spoken.

3. Begin to slowly align your behaviors with your truth, regardless of how it feels.

4. If the truth involves communicating a difficult message, make certain that message is clear, sensitive, and not framed in the form of blame or attack.

5. If you elect not to speak your truth—and because you're human, you'll make this choice at times—fully accept the consequences.

CHAPTER
FIVE

L I F E L E S S O N

Can You Lead with Heart?

Great leadership doesn't require lofty positions. Leadership is the degree to which you are willing to influence those around you. You do not need the title of "leader" to be a leader. Some of the most influential people of our time did not have leader titles. The key to great influence is your values. What do you value most? To what extent do you exercise your influence in places and in ways that make a difference and are aligned with your core values? You can't influence others if you aren't clear about that. If you allow distractions at work and at home to influence your decisions, they can easily sidetrack you.

Most organizations get into trouble when the leaders of those organizations begin to compromise their values. I know many organizational leaders who say they are committed to making decisions based on their core values, but when push comes to shove, they sacrifice those values in service of the bottom line. If there is unrest in the organization where you work or in your life personally, I can guarantee you, you are dealing with a values conflict. It takes courage and heart to be true to what matters. If you, or your organization, are not living in alignment with a set of sound core values, profit won't fix it. New offices won't fix it. A happy board of directors won't fix it. A new job won't fix it. Pretending definitely won't fix it! The only thing that *will* fix it is courage—the courage to do whatever it takes to live in alignment with your core values.

If you are a leader of an organization, do your people rigorously adhere to a clear set of values? If you don't have them identified, get a group together and identify them. If you do have established values but they are just a nice poster on the wall, get busy establishing a plan for full and rigorous implementation.

If you are a parent, it's just as important to have a clear set of values that your kids buy into and follow. Yes, a family is an organization, too, and the principles that help it thrive are really not that different.

I am often asked if it is more important to have your core values identified for home or for work. This question scares me. Your values are your values, plain and simple. It is never a good idea to change them based on where you are. Doing so sets a confusing precedent, unless of course one of your values is making everyone happy and changing who you are for the group you are in. I hope this is not the case. If it were, you probably wouldn't be reading a book like this in the first place.

These steps will help you determine your core values:

Answer the following questions:

1. What do you value most?
2. How do you know?
3. What are you going to do to drive those values into the organization's culture or deeper into your daily life?

If you are in an organization that is not values-based and is not living by a clear and purposeful set of values, then:

1. Determine how much energy you are willing to invest to change it.

2. If you aren't willing to do anything, then ask yourself: *What am I valuing that allows me to stay here?*

3. Find ways to invest energy in places where you are living in alignment with what really matters.

Think of it this way, would you be willing to follow and trust a person with shaky values? Absolutely not! Don't be that kind of person, either.

CHAPTER
SIX

L I F E L E S S O N

Do You Consider Unintended Consequences?

Few people in the world wake up in the morning and say to themselves, "I'd like to make a really stupid decision today." But have you ever made a decision and found that certain things happened as a result that you wish *hadn't* happened? Ever said something and discovered later that your words were misinterpreted? I am suggesting that we always consider the unintended consequences of our choices.

Unintended consequences are not always negative. For example, many lifesaving medicines have come about because of unintended consequences. In business and in our personal lives, there are consequences to the actions we take and the words we say. Careful consideration of them on every level will help you avoid mistakes. Yes, it is impossible to eliminate mistakes, but if you consider the possibility of other (unwanted) potential outcomes, you can plan for those as well.

The important thing to remember is that whenever strong emotion gets involved, it tends to blind us to potential outcomes of our actions, both good and bad. Reach for the cool voice of logic and *force* yourself to consider all aspects of your decision. If that is difficult to do, seek counsel from a friend or trusted advisor. Try to avoid hearing yourself say, "Hmmm...I didn't think of that!"

Here is how to do that:

1. Always be certain about what you *intend* the outcome to be.
2. Ask yourself, "What *could* happen that I haven't really thought about?"
3. To the extent you are capable, have a plan to manage those unintended consequences.
4. Remember, the more emotional you are about a decision (big or small), the more important it is to consider unintended consequences.

CHAPTER
SEVEN

L I F E ✓ L E S S O N

Do You Tend to Be Frank or Diplomatic? (You Can Be Both!)

Being able to communicate effectively is probably the most important skill a person can have. My hope is that you are both frank and diplomatic. One does not preclude the other. People who are effective both personally and professionally know how to blend these seemingly paradoxical communication styles. It's the key to being an outstanding communicator.

Frankness has to do with how clear you are, while diplomacy has to do with how tactful you are. Which way do you tend to fall? Most people mistakenly think that in order to increase one trait you must decrease the other. Not true. If you tend to be more frank than diplomatic, then your work should center on increasing diplomacy, not decreasing frankness. All outstanding communication is a blend of the two.

It is possible to be a great talker and a poor communicator. An excellent communicator is aware of not only *what*, but *how*, to communicate. When people find themselves in communication trouble, it is generally less about the message and more about the delivery. When you are "brutally frank" with someone on a sensitive subject—about poor job performance, say, or the need for weight loss—your lack of diplomacy may lead to an outcome opposite of what you intended. Understanding your tendencies will allow you to make the appropriate adjustments.

Here is how to be certain you are balancing "frank" and "diplomatic":

1. Evaluate your tendencies. Which way do you lean—toward frankness or diplomacy?

2. Develop skills that increase the weaker element. Do not reduce the stronger element. If you tend to be more frank than diplomatic, do not attempt to become less frank. Instead, drive the opposing side of the paradox up by trying to become more diplomatic.

3. Ask a friend, family member, or colleague to evaluate your progress.

CHAPTER
EIGHT

Can You Be Still?

I saw a commercial that had the line, "Sure, you are active, but why?" Good question! I encourage you to learn to be still. If you are like most people, you are very busy. Think of all the times you have been asked how you are doing and you have answered, "Busy." But perpetual busyness, like anything else taken to excess, can be counterproductive. It can throw your body, mind, and spirit out of balance.

Eleanor Roosevelt once said, "Don't just do something—stand there!" The most successful people I know have mastered the ability to be still. I have found that my most productive moments come with stillness. Whether you're at work or "relaxing" at home, your mind does not need the frantic voltage you expose it to in order to be successful.

Stillness does not necessarily involve sitting quietly at the feet of some monk in a mountain hideaway. It is about a mindset and a willingness to approach stillness physically, emotionally, mentally, and spiritually. The most effective way to get more of what you want, and less of what you don't want, is to commit to stillness on a regular basis.

Here's what I suggest:

1. Intentionally set aside time to be still every week (put it on the calendar, or it won't get done). Start with half an hour; you can add more time later if you desire.

2. Find a place where you won't be disturbed and won't fall asleep. (I go to the water.)

3. Turn off your cell phone, BlackBerry®, Treo™, etc.

4. Give yourself time to think about some area of your life. Don't analyze it to death—just be still. This can feel uncomfortable sometimes because we are not conditioned to be still. Maybe your time should be spent observing something in your environment: a plane flying over or a bird on a branch, for instance. Or it may involve being with thoughts about a job change or a relationship. The most important thing is that you avoid trying to *make* something happen.

5. Be patient. It will take about one month before you really experience results.

CHAPTER NINE

L I F E ✓ L E S S O N

Do You Follow the Golden Rule? I Hope Not!

Anyone who knows me well is aware that I do not like or believe in clichés. Most people say things meaning well but often do not stop to consider the impact (or lack thereof) of their words. The golden rule—*Do unto others as you would have others do unto you*—is just such an example. The golden rule works only if other people want to be treated the way you like to be treated. Guess what? They *don't* always. To give a simple example, maybe you're an outgoing "people person" who loves raucous surprise parties. That doesn't mean your quiet, introspective colleague would appreciate your throwing her one.

Too often our focus is on us and the assumption that everyone wants to be treated the way we do. It would be far better to "do unto people as they would have themselves done to." See the difference? I encourage you to fully embrace this idea, to understand others'

19

needs, and then to do everything in your power to help them be treated as they would like to be treated. Make this principle a part of your relationships at home and at work.

Here's how to do it:

1. Seek to find out how others want to be treated—what makes them feel appreciated, respected, and so forth.

2. Find direct and indirect ways to do things in a way that is aligned with what you discover.

3. Always look at the treatment of others through the lens of *them*—not the lens of *you*.

4. Be prepared for some shocked people in your life.

5. Enjoy the positive outcome of being selfless enough to do what others find useful and constructive.

CHAPTER
TEN

Are You Really *Grateful?*

I am dedicating this chapter to gratitude. We live in a world that is so fast-paced and busy that few of us take the time to truly and deeply express gratitude. I am not talking about a polite "thank-you." I mean something deeper, a profound emotion that you take the time to feel and express. It takes courage to be open enough to let people know that you are grateful. Our entire culture, from advertising to therapy, is designed to convince you that life is all about you. Let me be clear: It is not all about you. I want you to take a look at your life and ask yourself a simple yet powerful question: Are you deeply grateful, and are you mindful enough to experience that gratitude and express it? Do not let another day pass without a real commitment to feeling and expressing it.

What do you think the world would be like if each of us committed to recognizing one person every day and expressing our gratitude to him or her? I challenge you to make a lifelong commitment to doing exactly that.

I created a club a few years back called the ROPED club. I am inviting you to join. It is free of fees but not free of responsibility.

ROPED stands for Recognize One Person Every Day. If you want to join, here are the rules: You **must purposefully** recognize one person every day *for the rest of your life*. It can be anywhere at anytime: the woman with the full shopping cart who lets you go ahead of her in line or the salesman who brings in the account you've been pursuing for years. Just do it. Our world is so fast and busy that people seldom receive recognition; you'll be amazed by how much it means to them.

Purposeful recognition is:

1. Specific—Be certain that the recognition addresses something the person did.

2. Appreciative—Be clear that it mattered to you!

3. Personal—Make it connected to the person, and, when possible, do it live!

4. Immediate—Don't wait! Do it as soon as possible!

CHAPTER ELEVEN

Who Should You Blame?

From the time we are very young, we engage in a game of blame. As a child, you probably answered your parents' questions about why you did something with "Everybody does it!" or "Because so-and-so did it!" or "So-and-so made me do it!" If you have kids of your own, you've probably heard the same words. And it's not only kids. How often do we hear adults blame their environment, the market, their significant other, their heredity, or some other entity for their problems?

I suggest that this is an enormous waste of energy and, in most cases, it doesn't matter who is to blame. I love this statement: "It's not your fault, but it is your problem!" I heard those words of wisdom from Doug at Long Realty Company who thinks it might have come from his coworker Theresa. I am not sure who to blame (or credit) for this phrase, but I like it! I would counsel you to forget who or what is to blame and get on with the business of dealing with the problem.

Here's how:

1. Accept the problem you're facing in all its fullness. Don't make mountains out of molehills or molehills out of mountains. Commit to rigorous reality.

2. Identify those parts of the problem you have control or influence over.

3. In those areas where you have control, make immediate changes.

4. In those areas where you have influence, meet with the person who does have control and state your case clearly. Ask specifically for what is needed to deal effectively with the problem.

5. Keep moving forward. Do not allow yourself to get trapped in the problem; move toward a solution or move on.

CHAPTER
TWELVE

L I F E ✓ L E S S O N

Are You Playing to Win or Are You Playing Not to Lose?

In many ways, we have let the pendulum swing too far in the "can't-we-all-just-get-along" direction. While I think it is a good idea to look out for each other and to live in alignment with our values, I think it's an exceptionally bad idea to play things too conservatively. Life rewards action. Sometimes you have to step out of your comfort zone and take a risk.

I encourage you to ask yourself: *Am I playing to win...or am I merely playing not to lose?* Playing to win involves balancing your willingness to take risks with your ability to look at the downside of those risks. Playing not to lose involves being cautious to a fault. It is generally driven by the fear of losing—losing a job, a relationship, a big contract, a client, a reputation. Less concretely, it could mean losing your sense of security or certainty.

Playing to win is about being forward-thinking and forward-acting such that you are willing to charge hell with a squirt gun, if necessary, to accomplish what you need to accomplish.

Here are the steps I suggest for ensuring that you are playing to win:

1. Make decisions with an attitude of determination and courage.

2. Focus attention on the desirable result and avoid the "what-ifs."

3. Be bold.

4. Be persistent, especially when the obstacles are big.

5. Move further out on the limb than you feel comfortable with, but not so far as to be careless.

6. Surround yourself with people who will push you, not restrain you with *their* fear.

CHAPTER
THIRTEEN

Are You Paying Attention?

I am always surprised by how inattentive people can be. When I was in college, we did an experiment in my Psych 101 class. We were instructed to respond with an enthusiastic "Bad, thanks!" when asked "How are you?" I, along with the rest of the class, was amazed that far more than 80 percent of the people met my "Bad, thanks!" with an automatic response like "Great, have a good day!"

People just don't pay attention. In a store the other day, I watched a very frustrated little kid (five years old or so) attempt to get his mother's attention. Finally, in a gasp, he yelled, "Jennifer!" apparently employing her first name for shock effect. Are *you* like that harried mother? Here is a checklist to determine just how well (or how poorly) you do at paying attention.

Try these 15 statements on for size:

- ✔ I approach important situations without clearing my mind or taking steps to prevent interruptions or distractions.
- ✔ I engage in other activities while I'm "listening" (opening mail, watching TV, etc.).
- ✔ I assume I know what others will say.
- ✔ I interrupt.
- ✔ I finish sentences for people.
- ✔ I become impatient and tune others out when they say things I don't agree with or don't want to hear.
- ✔ I form a rebuttal or response in my mind while they talk.
- ✔ I ignore non-verbal cues such as tone, voice, or body language.
- ✔ I act as if I understand when in fact I don't.
- ✔ I listen for specific facts rather than broad ideas.
- ✔ I fidget when people speak too slowly.
- ✔ I dwell on aspects of the speaker (clothing, mannerisms, etc.) that have no bearing on the content of her words.
- ✔ I daydream while others are talking.
- ✔ I use repetitive responses (uh huh, right, etc.).
- ✔ I use body language that discourages communication.

I challenge you to choose one of the items you checked off and commit to *not* doing it for the next week. You will be amazed at how hard it is—and at how effective you will become once you master the habit of listening.

CHAPTER
FOURTEEN

L I F E ✓ L E S S O N

What Do You Think About When Times Are Tough?

Every day we are faced with challenges in our personal and professional lives. These challenges are sometimes controllable, at least to some degree, but often are not. Think of it this way: You are either dealing with a difficult issue now, or are about to, or have just finished dealing with one. Now, don't you feel better? My point is that challenges are everywhere, and to weather them, you must not let them steal your attention.

Your success has everything to do with where your focus is. The brain is designed for only one purpose...to keep you alive! Any time the mind feels threatened, it wants to focus on that threat. This makes sense if the challenge is a hungry saber-toothed tiger lurking outside your cave, but not so much if it's an irate client wanting to know why last month's invoice was 20 percent higher than usual. Non-life-threatening challenges don't warrant constant fretting.

I am not suggesting that you adopt a value of carelessness, but rather that you change where you spend your thought energy. *Don't* minimize the reality of life's difficulties. *Do* approach challenges with balanced thinking and appropriate focus. I have found that people who do well in the tough times are not necessarily the stronger ones or the smarter ones. Those who travel through the valleys successfully tend to have their minds set on certain things. Whether the challenge you're facing is as simple as not getting a sale you really needed or as major as a death in your family, it doesn't have to de-rail you.

Here are five things to think about when times are tough:

1. Family and friends are long-term; money is short-term.

2. One good opportunity will change the entire direction of your circumstances.

3. Spend 90 percent of your time focused on the opportunities and 10 percent of your time focused on solving the problems.

4. Focus on what you are becoming—not on what you are or on what you were.

5. Schedule a fixed amount of time each day to deal with challenges. Once that time is over, *move on* to the things that will move you past the challenging time.

CHAPTER
FIFTEEN

L I F E ✓ L E S S O N

Obstacles *or* Opportunities? *Where Is Your Focus?*

We live in a real world with real problems that are really challenging. It is foolish to attempt to dilute that reality with cheesy clichés or platitudes. The fact is, Nietzsche was wrong: It is not always true that "what doesn't kill us makes us stronger." It is not always true that "every cloud has a silver lining." But it is true that where we focus our energy and behavior has a significant impact on our results.

I want you to ask yourself a simple question: Am I opportunity-focused or obstacle-focused? When faced with business or personal challenges, do you focus your attention on those things that are in the way, or do you see the opportunity in spite of the obstacles? *Careful*...this is a trick question! It is best if you focus on both obstacles and opportunities, but with a stronger focus on the opportunity. A wise person channels energy into the opportunity with a plan for how to overcome or avoid the obstacles.

Do not cling to empty platitudes or clichés! Focus your energy on those things that move you forward. Force movement against the grain when the grain seems to indicate that you should give up. Yes, the road is difficult. Forge ahead anyway! Learning to balance perseverance with a willingness to change is critical to ensuring the greatest opportunity for success.

Five steps to eliminate (or at least reduce) obstacles:

1. Every day there are opportunities and obstacles...acknowledge that!

2. Choose to invest energy in those opportunities that have a high probability of a positive rate of return.

3. Acknowledge and evaluate the obstacles: Can you change or eliminate them, can you influence them, or should you avoid them?

4. Eliminate "buts" and excuses, replacing them with a plan of action.

5. Adjust your strategy as needed.

CHAPTER
SIXTEEN

L I F E ✓ L E S S O N

Why Are Shoulds *So Bad for You?*

A *should* is simply an expectation imposed (emphasis on "imposed") by us on another person, on some set of circumstances, or on ourselves. The reason *shoulds* are so bad for you, your family, and your work is that they are usually irrational or, sometimes, actively toxic. Now before you go getting all uptight because you assume I am supporting an amoral lifestyle, hear me out.

If you live your life based on *shoulds*, you will usually find yourself more frustrated and less productive. "Lisa should perform better," "Bob should drive better," "Francine should be nicer," and on and on it goes! Buying into *shoulds* causes us to create unrealistic or irrational expectations for ourselves and for those around us. Who says Lisa should perform better? What rule is written that Bob should drive better? And Francine should be "nicer" by whose standards? Scrapping the *shoulds* requires a simple shift in the words we use and the way we think. The smallest changes in our behavior often lead to the most significant results. Believing that there is only one way to see the world and that way is your way creates a mindset that leads to frustration. *Should* is always our attempt to impose our beliefs and rules on ourselves and on the world around us.

Challenge every *should* you come across. The easiest way to do so is to replace your *shoulds* with other more rational and appropriate words, such as "*It would be better for the company if* Lisa performed at a higher level," "*I would prefer it if* Bob drove better," or "*It would be easier* to deal with Francine if she smiled more often." Gas prices are up and the country is at war; there is no reason to allow yourself to be involved in any more bad news. *Shoulds* always lead to an unnecessary expenditure of energy!

Here are three steps to eliminate the *shoulds* from your vocabulary:

1. Pay attention to where and when you most often use *shoulds*.

2. Challenge yourself to eliminate them by stopping yourself and changing your speech pattern anytime you notice a *should* coming up.

3. Replace your *shoulds* with phrases like *I would prefer it if, It would be better if,* or *I would like it if*—anything but a *should* or a *must*.

CHAPTER
SEVENTEEN

L I F E ☑ L E S S O N

How Do You Deal with Change?

"Change is difficult." How many times have you heard this sentiment? Too many times, I'll bet. Here is a counter-statement that will make your life easier: Change is *not* difficult...unless and until you equate it with something dangerous or bad. Once your mind is convinced that something is going to be bad or dangerous, your brain literally triggers an alarm that causes you to repel the thought of it.

When I ask the question "What do you think scares people or makes them uncomfortable in times of change?" I generally hear this answer: "They're afraid of the unknown." Let's analyze that for a moment because, logically, it doesn't hold water. It is impossible to fear what you don't know. If something is *truly* unknown, the only thing you would feel is curiosity or ambivalence. One can fear only what they *think* they know. So discomfort with change is always the result of a negative prediction about an outcome that we think change will bring. We assume that something "bad" is going to happen; then we fear that (theoretical) outcome, in advance!

It doesn't make a lot of sense, does it? Here's the truth: Whether your market is changing, your relationship is changing, your health is changing, or your circumstances in general are changing, you will get through it. The way you get through it is what I want to help you with.

Discomfort, fear, or anxiety is always created by an *in*creasing sense or perception of danger and a *de*creasing sense of your ability to cope with that perceived danger. *So,* there are only two ways to deal with it: Decrease the sense of danger or increase your ability to cope.

That said, here are six key questions I'd like to challenge you with:

1. What is the worst thing that could happen?
2. What is the best thing that could happen?
3. What is the most likely thing that could happen?

Answering those three questions will immediately create a realistic sense of danger. Next, answer these three questions:

1. What will I do if the worst thing happens?
2. What will I do if the best thing happens?
3. What will I do if the most likely thing happens?

Anxiety must be decreased if the mind knows there is a specific coping plan. So no matter what changes you face in your life, deal with the threat first and the plan second.

CHAPTER
EIGHTEEN

L I F E ☑ L E S S O N

Are You Creating a World-Class Experience?

Please read the headline carefully. Then read it again. When all extraneous issues are stripped away, the experience you create for your customers is the single most critical factor in determining sustained success at work. Now, substitute *significant other* or *family* for "customers" and *home* for "work." In a very real sense, nothing else matters. How that experience is defined is your key to continuing to prosper.

I sometimes hesitate to speak of creating an experience because it can sound clichéd or overly simplistic. The fact is that up until around 1995, the experience didn't really matter that much with customers. (It has always mattered in relationships.) But when the Internet and globalism exploded onto the scene—bringing with them an endless supply of competition—suddenly, it mattered. A lot. To believe that customers are going to consistently transact business with you when you cling to old (non-customer-centric) strategies is to ignore the majority of the research and to ignore your own experience. Today the customer, and only the customer, defines what that experience is and how much it is worth.

Trying to get people to buy what they may or may not need—or in terms of personal relationships, to act in a way they may or may not want you to act—is to believe that you know more than them. When it comes to another person's needs, customer or otherwise, *you do not know more than them!* You must figure out what they really need or expect and determine the extent to which you are willing and able to deliver that.

My question to you is simply this: To what extent is your firm focused on making sure your customers have a world-class experience *as they define it?* Is your organization turning out slightly arrogant horn blowers for your brand, or thoughtful, self-effacing, customer-centric servants who get customers to promote your brand? Obviously, yours may be one of the firms that "gets it" and is doing everything right. But if you suspect you have some rethinking to do, I don't want you to feel overwhelmed. I like to advise my clients to do things in small, manageable steps. Momentum is the key to your success. Momentum channeled in the right direction leads to outstanding results.

Your relationships are successful for the exact same reasons. The experience you create for your partner, kids, and so on will have much to do with the success of these relationships as well. To what extent are you creating experiences for your significant relationships that lead to fulfilling and uplifting living?

Don't forget your employees, either. To what extent does your workplace stimulate experiences that are uplifting, compelling, and energy-creating? I encourage you to evaluate *all* areas of your life and determine how successful you are at creating world-class experiences.

The three steps to effectively creating the exceptional experience are:

1. Assessment. Immediately do an assessment to determine the extent to which every element of the experience is centered on the customer's expectations. Talk to a cross-section of customers, and with each one, strive to determine:

   - Is the process of dealing with you simple?

   - Are you adding value with every transaction or interaction?

   - Does the customer understand the value as it relates to the price?

   - How quickly are you recovering from a failure to deliver on the experience?

2. Intervention. Once you have assessed the circumstances, create a clear plan of alignment. Align your behavior with the customer's expectations to the extent that it is within your values and capability. Do not let *your* level of comfort dissuade you from changing. It's not about your comfort; it's about theirs.

3. Follow-up. Charge someone in the organization with monitoring progress. You should be constantly aware of how closely the organization is aligned with the desired outcome. It is about decreasing complexity and increasing efficiency in the experiences you provide. Check in with those you are centering the experience on to see how they evaluate the experience and whether you're succeeding.

These same three steps can be modified to create better experiences with other (non-customer) people in your life as well. Get started! As your relationships improve, so will the quality of your own life experiences.

CHAPTER
NINETEEN

Can You Follow the Only Known Formula for Success?

(Hint: It's Intention + Resilience.)

Most of us have good intentions. We intend to lose weight; we intend to stop smoking; we intend to get out of debt. Many of those intentions turn to hopes, which later turn to rationalizations. Herein lies the problem. The perplexing gap between intentions and behavior is what gets most organizations and individuals in trouble. Closing the gap requires discipline and certainty. Effective people and organizations do not measure themselves only by how often and quickly they close the intention gap, but by how resilient they are in making the necessary adjustments and taking the right risks.

Setbacks are inevitable in life and work. *Do not* think for one second that you have *the* strategy for success. There is only one formula I know of for success, and it can be summed up in two principles: 1. leading and living intentionally and 2. becoming resilient.

Leading and living intentionally means that you do not allow the natural progression of events to guide your every move. If your marketplace is strong, do not think that will continue without intentional intervention on your part. All winning streaks end. Making deliberate choices and focusing purposefully on the next steps will assist you in closing the gap between intention and reality.

Resilience has to do with being flexible and pliable in the way you deal with the world around you. It also has to do with pressing forward even when the odds are against you. To what extent are you able to be flexible in your approach to life and work? How pliable are you when things start to move in an undesirable direction? How resilient are you?

Here are six steps to get you started applying the only known formula for success:

1. Be absolutely clear about what your expected results are and what you are pursuing.

2. Be clear about why those results are important to you and how you will benefit from them. Keep that in the forefront of your mind.

3. Surround yourself with people who support you and will hold you accountable.

4. Recover quickly from failure. Do not rest too long before you get back in the fight.

5. Remember to change your strategy. Don't keep trying something that is not working, but also don't give up just because the heat is on.

6. Celebrate incremental successes. It will keep you motivated.

CHAPTER
TWENTY

Do You Align Your "Want-Tos" with Your "Willing-Tos"?

Most of us (and don't admit it if you don't) have good intentions. We *want* things to be a certain way, and we don't mind complaining when they aren't. Don't *you* do this? You say you want your company/department/personal productivity to improve; you say you want less stress in your life; you say you want to be in better shape; you say you want to have a successful relationship, and so on and so on. But the big question is: *Are you* willing *to?* Are you willing to do what's necessary to transition your wants to tangible results?

The incongruity that exists between your "want-tos" and your "willing-tos" is the difference between actually getting the results you seek and living in a state of frustration. It takes an enormous amount of energy to live in the gap between want-tos and willing-tos. The myth is that it is easy to bridge that gap. It is not. It takes hard work and focus. I am suggesting that, perhaps, you might need to do some serious alignment work. I am not suggesting that everything you want you should have. I am not even suggesting that if you could get it you should. What I am encouraging you to consider is this: *Are you* really *willing to do the things necessary to* really *get the want-tos?*

If you want more income, are you really willing to do what must be done to get it? Bill Bacharach had a huge impact on our company by saying one simple phrase to me at a conference once: "If you want X, you have to do the work, whatever that work is!" How obvious is that? Do the work! Someone recently said to me, "My want-tos motivate me." The only time a want-to motivates is when one makes a decision to *do* something with the want-to. Otherwise, it's just a wish.

I was recently speaking with a client and listened as she rattled off five very specific want-tos about her business. When I asked her if she was willing to do what was necessary, it stopped her in her tracks. It turned out that she wasn't willing to *at all*. The interesting thing was the freedom she felt when she was able to let go of the not-willing-tos and focus her energy only on those want-tos she really was willing to do the work to accomplish.

Here are some steps to help you close the gap:

1. Make a comprehensive list of your want-tos (i.e., *I want to have more money; I want to achieve greater success; I want to have a successful relationship; I want to feel better*, and so forth). On a scale of 0 to 10—with 10 being the most intense level of wanting and 0 being not wanting at all—rate each want-to.

2. Go through the list and ask yourself a simple question: *Am I willing to invest the time, energy, and resources necessary to have that want-to?* On a scale of 0 to 10—with 10 being *I am absolutely willing* and 0 being *I am not at all willing*—rate your degree of willing-to as it corresponds to each want-to.

3. Once that is complete, focus maximum energy on the want-tos that have the closest scores with your willing-tos.

4. Take your top three items and move the others off your list for now. Then, create a plan of action. Review your list every three to six months because your want-tos and willing-tos are constantly changing.

5. Stop making excuses and get to work.

   a. Get the support.
   b. Find the resources.
   c. Do the work.

6. Enjoy the success that comes with alignment between your want-tos and willing-tos.

CHAPTER
TWENTY-ONE

L I F E ☑ L E S S O N

What's So Powerful About Gifts?

Birthdays, anniversaries, and holidays are all about the joy of giving. At least, they should be. We all know that "giving" can sometimes turn into a frantic focus on urgency and a generous helping of "I-*must*-find-the-right-gift!" anxiety. Too bad. True gift giving is a powerful experience for both the giver and the givee. I want to encourage you to be mindful of what you have to give and what you need to receive, not just on special occasions but all year long.

In whatever roles you fill at home and at work, ask yourself: *Am I leveraging my influence in such a way that I am getting the maximum return on my unique gifts?* Well? What is it you do best? Perhaps you have the gift of communication and your direct reports would benefit from a renewed focus on clearing the low-gain clutter that the day seems to bring. Channel your energy into areas that will give you and the recipients of your gifts the best chance of reaping outstanding results.

On the other side of the coin, what gifts do you need to receive? What is it that you need more of or less of? There is a direct correlation between your ability to accurately assess what you need to perform at your peak and your satisfaction personally and professionally. Maybe you need to carve out a specific time in your week, every week, to consider what needs to happen to decrease complexity and increase efficiency in your life and work.

Most people get so busy working *in* their jobs that they do not take the time to work *on* their jobs...and their lives. Be mindful. Think through the unique gifts that you bring to those you influence at work and at home. And think about the gifts you can give to yourself.

Here are several ideas that will help:

1. Carve out time to be still and consider what you need to get and what you need to give at home and at work so that you—and not a BlackBerry, Palm Pilot, person, or some other urgency-producing element—are running your life.

2. Focus on activities that increase efficiency and decrease complexity at work and at home.

3. Set clear boundaries.

4. Eliminate the words "have to" from your vocabulary.

CHAPTER
TWENTY-TWO

L I F E ✓ L E S S O N

What Do You Stand For?

Some time ago I asked a client that question. He was surprised at how difficult it was to come up with an answer. Yet, when I asked him what his sales numbers were the previous month, he was able to recite them without a second thought. Can you relate to this scenario? Is how you make your living more important than what you're living for? Certainly not! *Both* issues are important. In order to live a life of balance and productivity, you must have a good grasp on both—but you must never forget which one matters most.

In a world that is flying by at ever-increasing speed, I encourage you to stop this week and answer the first question: *What do I stand for?* At the core of who you are, what is most important? Understanding what you believe—what your core values are—is the most important question you will ever answer. It is so much more important than what you do for a living or the tasks you complete each day.

Introspection is at the heart of outstanding performance in life and in work. Your willingness and ability to look inward and ask the difficult questions reveals the degree to which you are focused on the things that are most important. Once you have answered that key question, the second one to answer is: *To what degree are you living your life, at home and at work, in alignment with those values?*

By the way, I do not have any judgment about what the right and wrong values are for you. Despite what certain people tell you, your values and beliefs are yours alone and are very personal. However, you do need to know what they are!

Here are six steps to clear values alignment:

1. Identify what your core values and beliefs are—not what you think they should be, but what they actually are.

2. Write them down. Then put them aside for a few days.

3. At the end of a couple of days, ask yourself to what extent you are living and working in alignment with those values.

4. Make the necessary adjustments to your behaviors and where you spend your time and energy.

5. Eliminate excuses.

6. Filter *all* decisions through the prism of your values.

Practice these steps and adapt them to your everyday living. Then, if someone asks you the question we started with—*What do you stand for?*—you'll be able to answer with clarity and confidence.

CHAPTER
TWENTY-THREE

L I F E LESSON

Do You Know How to Survive the Storms of Life?

As I was watching CNN during the aftermath of Hurricane Katrina, I was amazed at how many different responses the survivors of storms exhibit. Some turn to the darkest side of their character while others rise above the trauma with attitudes of hope and helping. The responses are as varied as the number of people affected.

Living in Florida keeps me vigilant about my own appointment with "the big one," much like I imagine living in California would earthquake-wise. It is always good to be prepared. Most of us will never encounter a natural disaster the magnitude of Katrina, but all of us will face personal and professional "storms" that can have a devastating impact. As we face these storms, we get to choose how to handle them.

Using the Saffir-Simpson Hurricane Scale, meteorologists can determine the wind speed and flooding a hurricane will create.

Category One is the least powerful, while Category Five is the most devastating. Remember, however, a hurricane is still a hurricane. Category One storms are not just passing thunderstorms. They are real and they have impact. The same is true of the storms we face in life. When we practice handling smaller magnitude storms with grace and courage, we'll be better equipped to handle the big ones.

Take these five steps the next time you find yourself in a storm:

1. **Accept the fact that you will face storms in life.** You will face some Category One storms, at least one Category Five storm, and a few in-between. That is not some doomsday scenario; it is simply a fact of life. If you refuse to accept that storms will come, when the storms do come, you will be caught unprepared. Acceptance does not mean approval. Acceptance means acknowledging it and agreeing to face it. Acceptance also means saying, "I am in a storm." Do not use some psychobabble load of garbage to convince yourself that you are not in a storm. Those who refuse to face reality stand to sustain significant damage.

2. **Take responsibility for dealing with the storm and its consequences.** Ultimately, you and I are responsible for the choices we make. We live in a culture that constantly bombards us with the opportunity to blame someone or something else. Take responsibility for what is yours and let others take responsibility for what is theirs. There is no greater freedom than knowing what is yours and doing something with it. You are a hostage to the person or group that you blame. Don't take responsibility for more—or less—than what is yours.

3. **Take action that is appropriate and timely.** Sometimes you must sit still and ride out the storm; other times you must do something quickly. Decide what to do by evaluating what will be the highest-gain activity. The highest-gain activity is always the activity that stands to have the biggest impact in the shortest period of time. The bigger the storm, the longer the recovery. Be still and *never* make a life-changing decision in a moment of high emotional intensity.

4. **Acknowledge progress.** Sometimes the storms of life are so difficult that we long for the way things used to be. A sense of "normal and comfortable" seems so distant. Remember that the storm always passes and a "new normal" emerges. It may last a while and it may leave a mess, but the storm itself will pass. It may never be the way it used to be, but it will pass. Pay attention to the progress you are making on the road forward and celebrate the incremental gains.

5. **Find a safe place and have courage.** In business and in our personal lives, it is important to find a safe haven. If you are a leader in an organization, make certain you have a confidant or coach. Make sure there is somewhere to go that is safe and provides shelter so that you can think through what you need to do next. Personally, be certain that you are in the presence of and connected to those you trust and care about. In a hurricane, isolation is dangerous. In life, it is equally dangerous. Be courageous!

CHAPTER
TWENTY-FOUR

L I F E  L E S S O N

How Clear Are Your Boundaries?

One of the keys to driving performance in an organization or in your personal life is the ability to set appropriate boundaries. A boundary, for the purpose of this chapter, is simply an expectation— how you expect a person to perform at work or to treat you personally. Most challenges we face in life have something to do with how we set or do not set appropriate boundaries. Generally, people create challenges for themselves because their boundaries are too rigid or too flexible. The worst problems of all come when there are no boundaries.

You know your boundaries are too rigid if you hear yourself using words like "never," "always," "no matter what," and so forth. If they are too loose, you'll hear yourself say things like "I really just like to play things based on whatever is happening at the time." Either extreme is risky. Be cautious if you are setting (or not setting) boundaries based on emotion.

Establishing clear boundaries does two things: First, it eliminates ambiguity about how you expect a person to perform or treat you. Second, it gives you a sound measuring benchmark by which to evaluate performance and relationships.

Consider the following questions when establishing or clarifying boundaries:

1. What are my expectations (at work regarding performance, at home relative to how I expect people to treat me)?
2. Which behaviors annoy me but I'll tolerate?
3. Which behaviors are not okay, and I will confront?
4. Which behaviors are such a violation of my boundaries and expectations that the person will be eliminated from the company or my life?

Be certain that you are saying "yes" to the things you need to say "yes" to and "no" to the things you need to say "no" to. Most challenges in life come from saying "yes" when we should say "no" and saying "no" when we should say "yes."

Now go set some boundaries!

CHAPTER
TWENTY-FIVE

L I F E ✓ L E S S O N

Where's Your Courage?

Never make a life- or business-altering decision in a moment of high emotional intensity. When that emotion is fear or anxiety, be especially wary. There have probably been more regrettable decisions driven by what we are afraid of than by any other emotional state.

Fear manifests when you think about what will happen or what won't happen in a particular situation. Anxiety and fear are *always* the result of making a catastrophic prediction about the future. You cannot ever be afraid of the unknown. If it is unknown, you can't fear it. You can be afraid or anxious only about what you *think* is going to happen. I have seen more opportunities missed as a result of that insidious emotion than any other. I am not speaking here about the fear of things that are *really* dangerous; I mean fearing something that is not actually a threat to our physical being.

Most fear boils down to one question, and that question is: "What if?" *What if I fail? What if it doesn't work out? What if we don't hit the numbers? What if... what if... what if?* You must battle the tyranny of the "what-ifs." Fear begins when your mind believes there is an increasing sense of danger and a decreasing sense of your ability to cope. Courage as an acronym is **C**ontinuing **O**nward

Under **R**igorous **A**nd **G**rinding **E**xperiences. In order to continue onward, you must answer the question "What if?"

Of course, "What if?" is only one question to ask yourself.

Here are some others that will help you continue onward under rigorous and grinding experiences:

1. Have I ever handled or experienced anything even remotely similar to this?

2. What did I do or avoid doing that helped me deal with it?

3. Have I managed to get through *every* single event that has ever happened to me?

4. What is the likelihood I will get through every event that will ever happen to me?

5. What would be the most courageous and rational thing I could do right now to move my life and work ahead?

Then, once you've answered number five, act...regardless of how you feel.

CHAPTER
TWENTY-SIX

L I F E ☑ L E S S O N

What Does It Take to Maintain an Optimistic Focus?

I am in the middle of writing a book titled *When Life Hands You Lemons, They're Still Sour; I Don't Care What You Make of Them.* That sums up my belief about cheesy clichés designed to smooth over the very trying events that each of us experience. Sometimes bad things happen and denying that you're standing there holding a big bag of sour lemons serves no purpose. However, it is possible to face reality and still maintain an optimistic focus.

Maintaining an optimistic focus has everything to do with how you explain the events of life to yourself, and little, if anything, to do with the event itself. The stores are overflowing with books that promise quick fixes to almost every problem a human being can face. Sometimes it just isn't that easy.

59

Positive and negative events happen to both the optimist and the pessimist. No one is born an optimist or a pessimist. We were taught to think and react the way we do.

In his book *Learned Optimism: How to Change Your Mind and Your Life*, Dr. Martin Seligman clearly defines the difference between optimists and pessimists. He found in his research that the extent to which one is exposed to positive or negative life events has little to do with whether that person is optimistic or pessimistic. Neither does the severity of the events themselves. What makes the difference is how each individual interprets each event.

So, following Dr. Seligman's lead, the next time a negative event happens in your life, think of words that indicate the situation is temporary, specific to this time and place, and not a personal attack on you by God, the Universe, or Whomever. You can teach yourself to be more optimistic starting now. Just remember, optimism does not mean being happy all the time. Instead, think of it as a way to explain life's events more appropriately.

CHAPTER
TWENTY-SEVEN

L I F E  L E S S O N

Do You Know How to Handle Challenging People?

We all have people in our lives who are challenging. Most of these people don't think *they* are the ones who are challenging. You know the type. They are always making excuses for their difficult behaviors. They say things like, "This is just the way I am," or, "This is just my personality," and so forth.

Here's the thing: If these people can't (or won't) change themselves, you certainly can't do it for them. Instead, you must evaluate how much energy you are willing to invest in them. Making this determination will influence all of your subsequent behaviors.

Most people invest far too much energy in trying to change the difficult behaviors of others. Don't be one of them. It doesn't work, and it only makes you crazy.

The six key strategies to use when dealing with the difficult are:

1. Determine how much mental and emotional energy you are willing to invest in a particular person.

2. If you decide to invest your energy, then identify the specific behaviors that are difficult. Does she constantly interrupt? Is she condescending? Does she talk about you behind your back?

3. Address those behaviors in terms of quantity, using words like: *start* and *stop*; *begin* and *end*; *increase* and *decrease*; and *more* and *less*. For instance: "Please stop interrupting and let me finish."

4. As the person's behavior changes, acknowledge it immediately.

5. If the bad behavior does not change, evaluate how much energy you are investing and how much more you are willing to invest.

6. Once you can authentically look in a mirror and be clear that you have done all you can to deal with the difficult person, insulate or isolate yourself from her to the degree possible.

Here is a big heads-up: Even if she is family, there is no rule that says you must subject yourself to disrespectful behaviors. It really is your choice.

CHAPTER
TWENTY-EIGHT

How Do You Deal with Conflict?

Conflict is a fact of life. I have spent the majority of my life in conflict...well, not actually *in* conflict, but at least helping people through it. Even though I know how to handle conflict, it is not always easy for me. It is not easy for anyone. That's why it is important to remember that you aren't supposed to enjoy it. But there are steps you can take to make conflict less stressful.

First, let's define conflict. It boils down to this: *I want something and something is in my way.* There is a difference between a conflict and a disagreement. Disagreements do not have to be resolved because they are usually based on opinion. These include issues such as politics, religion, whether a movie is good or not, and so forth.

If you are in a disagreement and want out, here are your options:

1. Agree to disagree.
2. Change your position and agree with the person.
3. Seek a neutral expert source such as the Internet.
4. Argue for sheer entertainment value.

If you are involved in a real conflict, something that has an impact on your interests, then it must be resolved.

The six steps to dealing with conflict are:

1. Ask questions to clearly determine the other person's position.
2. Acknowledge his perception as being real to him.
3. Ask him for his thoughts about solutions. ("What would you suggest be done?")
4. Offer your suggestions about resolution.
5. Evaluate all solutions based on the degree to which the solutions will get both parties' interests met.
6. If at an impasse, seek third-party assistance.

Never attempt to resolve a conflict or any other issue in a moment of high emotional intensity. Be certain to work to understand the other person's state of mind and perception. Do not continue to push someone who refuses to work toward resolution. Find a more productive way to accomplish your goals.

CHAPTER
TWENTY-NINE

What Does It Take to Communicate with the Opposite Sex?

WARNING: This is a longer chapter than most in this book. I *strongly* urge you to read the whole thing. Be open to what you read here...it will make a huge difference in your communication...or you could rationalize away the whole thing and continue with the way you do things now. It's your call.

COMMUNICATING WITH THE OPPOSITE SEX
Or, things to remember so that Mike stays out of trouble:

1. We are talking about style and energy, *not* gender!
2. All men have both masculine and feminine energy in the way they communicate.

---

a. Men typically exercise the type of energy they use based primarily on what was reinforced when they were younger or what was most dominantly modeled in their life.

b. In *most* cases, men are conditioned by our culture to respond in stereotypically masculine ways, regardless of what self-help books attempt to convince them to do.

3. All women have both masculine and feminine energy in the way they communicate.

a. Women typically exercise the type of communication energy they use based on what was most enforced when they were children.

b. In *most* cases, women are conditioned by our culture to respond to conflict with their own tendencies, thus creating conflict for them. It is not necessary for women to be more like men. Attempting to is a great mistake that is often made.

Stick with me. It will make more sense in a minute...

REMEMBER, IT'S NOT ABOUT GENDER; IT'S ABOUT ENERGY.

WOMEN are motivated by the need to be respected and heard.

It is more important for women to be heard than it is for them to win. For a woman, winning is most often about getting heard, not about who is right. It is more important that she is respected than that she conquers or defeats her opponent. Women define respect very differently from men.

MEN are motivated by conquest and competition.

Men believe success is tied to winning and conquering; thus, they communicate as if it is a competition. Men interpret winning as being the one who feels the most powerful at the end of the interaction or the one who gets the most of what he wants. That can be as simple as the need to be right. It is more important to a man that he wins than that he is heard. Respect has to do with power, not listening or understanding.

Can you see a conflict building between most men and women?

So let's all accept two fundamental concepts:

1. Women talk more than men (a lot more).

<u>Men:</u> Give women the opportunity to talk as much as is necessary to feel heard and respected. Do this by actually being interested and asking questions. The biggest complaint women have about men is "They don't listen, and they don't communicate with me. When they do communicate, it is generally a lecture." So guys, *shut up* (I mean this in a loving way)! She most often doesn't need the kind of all-knowing help you believe you possess, so let go of the fantasy that you can always make it better in *your* way. You can't...just face it. Ask her what she most needs from you and break your back bending over backwards to do exactly that.

Women will always find a place where they are respected and heard. This is why so many more women than men go to a "rent-a-friend" (also known as a therapist). It is not because she is weak and needs the help more than you. Trust me, you could use a tune-up yourself sometimes. One of the worst things to say to a person communicating from feminine energy is, "How many times do we have to talk about this?" and its obnoxious cousin—any noise, grunt, or groan that indicates a lack of interest—is just as bad. She at least needs to know you have a pulse. *Warning:* If you try this stuff, she is likely to pass out or be suspicious; just stick with it and be sincere.

<u>Women:</u> Be aware that he has good intentions but often sees your communication as a cry for help in fixing a problem. *Do not stop communicating.* Assume positive intent and let him know what you need from him from the beginning. This will help him feel like he can win, and for a guy, that is critical! Guys are also generally under the impression that they already know what you need. This is part of their delusion. Do not grow weary in helping him understand what it takes for him to win with you. It is your job to help him win. Whenever possible, help his ego out (genuinely).

Since most men are not used to this, they will think you are taking some type of illicit substance. Just stick with it. Try this with your (male) boss or (male) significant other—it will work with both.

2. Men have big egos (big ones).

Women: Give men every opportunity to win. Note that I did *not* say to let him get away with things that are disrespectful. Giving men the opportunity to win and enjoy a stable ego is about helping him understand what it takes to win *with you*. The biggest complaint men have about women is "It doesn't matter what I do; it is *never* good enough." So ladies, *get off his back* (I mean that in a loving way)! He needs to know when he does a good job, and you need to find ways to help that process along.

Listen up, S P E L L it out for him. He cannot read your mind, nor should you expect him to. He will feel set up and like he is failing a test if he doesn't specifically understand what he needs to do. Telling him "You should just know that" does not motivate him. It makes him shut down and hide...from *you*.

Men will always find a place they can win...always. Trust me, the argument is not about taking out the trash; it is *always* about feeling like he is powerful. Most men want to feel appreciated for *what they do*. This is in stark contrast from women, who generally want to be respected for *who they are*. Try this with him: "Thank you, I really appreciate you for *doing* that." One of the worst things you can say to a man is "I can't believe you did that...what were you thinking?" Repeatedly letting him know how he failed is not helpful. The next worst thing is your friends knowing more about what works with you than he does.

Men: Be aware that she is not actually attempting to reduce you to insignificance. Her natural desire to be respected and heard is often manifested in repeated requests to have the trash removed. It is never about the trash. It is important that you understand this about yourself: You are likely to shut down and get quiet when faced with a challenge you cannot win. Contrary to your programming, shutting down will only make things worse. Adhere to this rule *unless* you are angry, at which time it is critical that you be quiet.

When she tells you what she needs, this is not some attempt to reduce you or control you. It is usually an attempt to feel respected and heard. She knows what she wants most of the time, so ask. *She is not kidding, and she is not less intelligent than you!* Listen up. She really means it when she says what works for her.

Women and Men: Even if you don't buy into all of this, the next time you find yourself in a conflict with the opposite sex, just try a couple of the techniques I've mentioned here. You just may find there really isn't a conflict there at all.

CHAPTER
THIRTY

L I F E ☑ L E S S O N

Can You Actually Stop and Get Focused?

This chapter is all about you! As the pace of life intensifies—and yes, it seems to grow more hectic every year—it is important to take time to focus. Often we get so busy living our lives that we don't take time to stop and take a look at where we *really* want to be. Usually, we're just trying to keep up, or worse, attempting to speed up to get ahead of the game. Consider this: If you were driving a racecar and you realized the lug nuts on your wheels were loose, I'm guessing you would rectify the problem by taking a pit stop and having them tightened. I don't believe the solution to that problem would be to drive faster!

Our culture perpetuates an attitude of urgency that is very contagious and sometimes dangerous. Burnout can happen only when the amount of energy you're investing does not get a reasonable rate of return. Don't let it happen to you.

In order to live an outstanding life and to create outstanding results:

1. Set aside (that means actually schedule) several hours each month to reflect on your business and personal life. Spend this time simply thinking about how things are progressing and to what extent you are heading in the direction that is right for you. Do not allow your work and personal life to get on autopilot.

2. Develop a purposeful plan of action. Make several *firm* decisions that keep you focused on what really matters for you at home and at work. We do not achieve the results we seek by accident. It is the result of choices—*conscious* choices!

3. Develop a "don't do" list. Much of our time and energy is wasted on those things that do not add value.

4. Commit to relentless improvement. That doesn't necessarily mean more activity, more work, or more time. Improvement can and often does mean *less* of these things.

5. Ask yourself: *What changes in behavior would be necessary for me to accomplish what I need to accomplish?*

CHAPTER
THIRTY-ONE

Are You Versed in the Art of "Thought Stinginess"?

Some years ago, I went to the doctor because I was concerned about my memory. The doctor, who was approaching retirement, said to me, "Son, I could make up some technical reason for your memory problem, but it's really very simple: You're just putting too much stuff in your head that doesn't matter and your brain isn't sophisticated enough to eliminate the right things—so it just gets rid of things randomly. Now, that'll be $100.00."

Wow, what a way to get a useful slap in the face! How much energy do we spend storing things in our minds that just don't matter? For most of us, the answer is probably "too much!" The good news is that cramming your mind full of trivial stuff is a bad habit that can be unlearned.

Here are five things you can do to get focused on what matters:

1. Identify and keep your mind on your values and on what is most important—not what feels like it *should* be most important.

2. Spend the majority of your time on high-gain activity. Remember, major on majors—minor on minors. Avoid getting lured by unproductive busyness or drama.

3. Invest your energy in people (at home and at work) who will give you the maximum rate of return in the long-run.

4. Continually evaluate whether or not the choices you are making, the actions you are taking, and the thoughts you are having are in alignment with your core values and with a sense of purpose.

5. Make changes in behavior accordingly.

Human beings have a tendency to make things complicated. Some think that keeping all the necessary elements of work and life in order requires complex formulas and years of intense thought. I would argue that it really gets down to a focus on fundamentals. So be jealous of your thoughts. Be stingy with what you allow yourself to store in your mind. Focus.

CHAPTER
THIRTY-TWO

L I F E ✓ L E S S O N

How Often Do You Really Apply the Fundamentals of Success?

Everyone talks about success. Books are written about it. Seminars teach us how to achieve it. On any given night of the week, there is someone selling a "new" way to become successful. I think the key to success is pretty simple. Now don't get all upset with me for apparently oversimplifying. I said the *key* to success is simple, not the implementation (which can, admittedly, be difficult). So here's the deal. There are three steps to focus on when pursuing success at anything:

First, get clear about the desirable results. What do you want more or less of? How will it look and feel when it is complete? *Do not* start thinking of *how* to do it! The power of choice is critical to your success. Choose the result you want and make an unwavering commitment to it. Get off the excuse train and buy a one-way "commitment" ticket to the results you seek. I know, I know, it's difficult and scary...blah, blah, blah. Make the decision; you will be amazed at how quickly you start moving toward the goal.

Second, you must determine the appropriate strategy. This step is about how you are going to achieve the results. What strategy will you use? What resources will you need? What steps need to be taken to move you in the appropriate direction?

Third, ask yourself this question: "If I were going to be successful, what would I need to do right now—today—to start moving in that direction?" Then do it. If it doesn't work, do something else. Richard Dreyfuss in the movie *What About Bob* advised his ridiculously neurotic patient to take "baby steps." I, too, advise baby steps (even for the non-neurotic). Action produces momentum and a result. Most failure is the result of a failure to act.

Whether you are the president or the janitor, the principles are the same. To recap:

1. Identify the results you want.
2. Determine the strategy.
3. Take action. If the results aren't achieved, change the strategy...but stay firm in your commitment to the results!

CHAPTER
THIRTY-THREE

L I F E ☑ L E S S O N

Do You Lead with Courage?

Judy House, the best boss I ever reported to, used to say to me, "Mike, the higher you move in an organization, the less freedom you have." I agree. I would also add that the higher you go, the less leeway you have to act in a less-than-courageous manner. (Cue the Cowardly Lion's "Courage" monologue from *The Wizard of Oz.*)

In any endeavor where you have people looking to you for leadership, they are watching you and waiting to see how you will respond in each situation you face. Courage is not just about living boldly; it's about the ability and willingness to take a stand and live that stand in the choices that you make.

If the people who work with you were given truth serum and asked to write down three words or phrases that best describe the experience of working with you, what would those words or phrases be? Would they reveal that you're a courageous leader? Or would they indicate that you're a waffling, wishy-washy blame shifter? Practice demonstrating courage and holding others accountable for living and working courageously in the culture we call work.

The five characteristics of a courageous leader are:

1. Stays focused on desired results and is unwavering in pursuing them.

2. Removes the obstacles that stand in the way of achieving these results.

3. Acts decisively and takes responsibility for the choices he or she makes.

4. Avoids excuses and the people who make them.

5. Listens openly and non-judgmentally.

If these characteristics don't describe you, take heart. You can become a courageous leader. Here are the action steps for doing so:

1. Clarify expectations in your mind first.

2. Communicate expectations that may be ambiguous.

3. Collaborate in setting specific and measurable performance standards.

4. Follow up to hold people accountable.

CHAPTER
THIRTY-FOUR

What Does It Take to Coach or Be Coached?

Coaching is a great way to help others maximize their potential and live productive, rewarding lives. Leaders inside companies function as coaches. So do parents. Indeed, anyone who helps other people discover and enhance their own skills and creativity may be thought of as a coach. That's why in this chapter I would like to make a few suggestions on how to effectively coach and how to effectively be coached.

If you are in a leadership role, one of your primary responsibilities is to coach your direct reports. It will make you a better leader, and it will add value to those you lead (that is, if you are good at it).

There are five steps to becoming a great coach:

1. Make sure your heart is in the right place. You must have a genuine desire for your direct reports to succeed and a commitment to assist in any way possible.

2. Identify, with your direct report, the desirable performance outcomes and goals, professionally and personally.

3. Evaluate the current state of her performance. To what extent is she performing at the desired level?

4. Set specific, measurable goals and then set specific target dates for achieving new levels of performance.

5. Hold her accountable by scheduling regular coaching meetings. I suggest once a quarter.

If you are a parent, consider how you might modify the above steps to use with your children. Obviously, the process is less structured and formal, but working with kids to set goals and then holding them accountable *is* a form of coaching. Why not give it a try?

Now, back to the workplace. Regardless of your position in an organization, it is your responsibility to get the coaching you need and deserve. The greatest athletes in the world seek out the best coaches to help them reap the rewards of their talents. You should do the same.

The five steps to acquiring an effective coach:

1. Identify a great coach. If your manager is not open to coaching you, then find someone who is. Be relentless.

2. Be open and receptive to feedback. Avoid even the slightest hint of defensiveness.

3. Be clear and specific about your goals, personally and professionally.

4. Get your coach to help you identify blind spots. Often there are areas that we are unaware of.

5. Set specific performance targets and be certain that you are held accountable.

Coaching is a critical part of achieving a high quality of life at work and at home. No matter how successful you are already, having a trusted coach will make the journey more rewarding and enjoyable.

CHAPTER
THIRTY-FIVE

L I F E ✓ L E S S O N

What's the Best Way to Deal with an Angry Person?

At some point in your life, you have come across an angry person. He was either angry with you, or he was angry about something else and you were in the way. Maybe you were listening to him as he vented about a situation he had to cope with. Whatever the case, you probably felt uncomfortable with his display of emotion. His anger may have even sparked anger in you. Whether anger manifests at work or at home, it can derail productivity if you don't know how to deal with it.

There are some things that you should know about anger. First, anger *never* happens because of an event. It happens because of what one believes about that event. See the difference? If a person is angry, he is thinking one—or two, or all—of three thoughts about the event: 1. This is unfair, 2. It is happening to me, and 3. It is out of my control. The stronger a person believes these thoughts about an event, the angrier he will become. In all the years I have studied anger, I have always seen it manifested as the direct result of one of those beliefs. In order for an angry person to calm down, he must perceive a sense of fairness, impersonalization, or control.

Here are the steps that you should always take when dealing with an angry person:

1. Stay calm yourself. Intentionally focus your energy on remaining calm. You can do this by breathing slowly and focusing more on the angry person than on your reaction. While you will never stay completely calm, you must stay calmer than him.

2. Let him talk unless he is attacking you.

3. Avoid responding with clichés or offering advice.

4. Ask good questions when the time is right. The best question is: "How can I be most helpful?"

5. Set good limits: "I get that you are mad, but you don't get to call me names."

6. If he is clearly out of control, forget everything you just read except the advice to stay calm yourself. Get away from the person until he calms down.

CHAPTER
THIRTY-SIX

How Generous Are You?

Generosity is an interesting concept. Traditionally, it has to do with the extent to which you are giving, charitable, kind, or big-hearted. I encourage you to really examine the role generosity plays in your life and work.

We live in a culture that is really centered on the individual. Commercials are *always* about you. It is not in the interest of the advertisers to convince you that if you buy their products you will *really* help someone else. There are those in my profession (and probably many other professions) who think the more focused on yourself you are, the better results you will achieve. I disagree. I strongly believe that the spirit of generosity, translated into daily action, leads to success.

I encourage you to think about generosity in a different light. The traditional definition is obvious. You already know if you are a giver or a taker. The context I am concerned about is generosity as it relates to your thoughts and your attitudes. To what extent do you give people room to be themselves? How generous are you with celebrating differences in others? How much space do you give those around you to express themselves as they see the world? Do your thoughts and attitudes reflect a generous, inclusive mindset, or are they narrow and limited in scope?

Five ways to become a more generous person:

1. Come from a place of curiosity. Learning is the key to understanding.
2. Understand that acceptance is not approval.
3. Separate what a person does from who a person is.
4. Stand up for acceptance of differences in those around you.
5. Teach and model generosity of heart and mind.

CHAPTER
THIRTY-SEVEN

L I F E ☑ L E S S O N

Do You See Things the Way They Are or the Way You Wish They Were?

So, do you see things the way they are or the way you wish they were? I was coaching someone recently who was making a *major* decision that was having a significant negative impact on others. She was absolutely convinced that it was the right decision regardless of the avalanche of information that indicated the choice was not a good one. She was seeing the world the way she wanted it to be, not the way it really was. I don't have the space here to talk about the positive elements of denial, but let's just say that the places where denial is a good thing (and yes, there *are* some) are limited.

I am suggesting that a rigorous commitment to reality is the best way to live your life. I am not in any way saying that you should become some doom and gloom predictor of bad news. In fact, for some of you "Eeyores" of the world, reality is much brighter than you think or act like it is. Do not be deceived: *All* of us—yes, that's right, *all* of us—have areas of our lives that we just do not see clearly. So if you are Hank or Heather Happy all the time, may I respectfully suggest you *get over it*. Conversely, if you are Ned or Nelly Negative, I suggest the same. Neither attitude is an appropriate response to reality.

Here is how to live in a place of rigorous commitment to reality:

1. Look at the facts, not the feelings. I am not suggesting that you get rid of feelings; just separate them from the facts.

2. Check those facts out with a couple of trusted people in your life. Do a reality check. Insist that they give you the raw reality of the situation you're facing.

3. Determine how much of what you discover is something you want to/are willing to change.

4. Focus only on those things you can change.

5. When all is said and done, place yourself in a mindset of acceptance and understand that acceptance is not surrender.

CHAPTER
THIRTY-EIGHT

Are You Vigilant and Disciplined?

I have been doing a lot of thinking lately about the concepts of *vigilance* and *discipline*. Vigilance has to do with awareness and attention. Discipline has to do with control and restraint. To get the results from life that we want requires a certain amount of both. Vigilance without discipline is simply insight without application. Discipline without vigilance creates rigidity and insensitivity. High levels of the two create high levels of effectiveness.

Your best chance of achieving the results you seek is to balance both vigilance and discipline. One of the marks of a highly emotionally intelligent person is the extent to which he is aware of his environment and the impact of his choices and behaviors on others. This level of self-awareness is difficult to achieve without help. Most people overestimate or underestimate themselves. It is difficult to see yourself clearly.

Here is how to achieve a good balance of vigilance and discipline:

1. Ask yourself these tough questions:

   a. What am I paying attention to that I shouldn't be?

   b. What am I not paying attention to that I should be?

2. Find someone you trust to ask you these tough questions:

   a. What are you avoiding?

   b. What do you need to believe?

   c. What are you pretending not to know?

3. Constantly evaluate the results, both tangible and intangible.

4. Pay attention to, but don't be controlled by, others' reactions to you.

5. Add emphasis to vigilance or discipline as you see results.

CHAPTER
THIRTY-NINE

L I F E ✓ L E S S O N

What Have You Learned Lately?

We have been conditioned for most of our lives that on some level we should be comfortable. If it's too hot, we should be cooler. If it's too cool, we should be warmer. And so forth. Don't get me wrong, I am as much about comfort as anyone. But there is a challenge that comes with the pursuit of comfort: Too much comfort creates laziness—mentally, physically, emotionally, and spiritually. In order to be in a space of learning, you must have a willingness to be uncomfortable.

Mental discomfort is commonly called *confusion*. Whenever confusion is present, you have the highest probability of learning something new. Look at it this way: When you are exercising, you are often uncomfortable because of the exertion. Yet, you accept the discomfort because it builds physical strength. Well, being present with and accepting of emotion begins to build emotional strength. And however uncomfortable you may be with the subject, evaluating how you have an impact on something bigger than you (and how that something impacts you) strengthens you spiritually.

Learning is how we as a species survive and, in some cases, thrive. The best part about learning is that it increases the number of things—facts, topics, ideas, situations, and so forth—that you are comfortable with. How uncomfortable are you willing to be? The answer to that question will determine how much you are willing to learn. How much you are willing to learn will determine how far you will go in life.

Here is how to be a learner:

1. Begin each day with a determination to learn something new.
2. Intentionally look for things to learn.
3. Find ways to apply even the most mundane things that you learn.
4. Accept confusion or discomfort as an indicator that you have arrived at the best moment to learn.
5. Constantly ask questions of yourself, others, and the world around you.
6. Be in a state of perpetual curiosity.
7. Share what you learned with someone else.

CHAPTER
FORTY

L I F E  L E S S O N

Is Honesty Really *the Best Policy?*

Have you ever had someone say something to you that upset you, made you mad, or otherwise hurt your feelings? When you pointed that out to her, did she say, "Well, I am just being honest!" And didn't that make you want to say, "Well, lie a little!"

Too often, people use honesty as a weapon. They believe that just because it is true, it ought to be spoken. They are wrong. Now, before I start getting e-mails from people who think I am condoning lies or misleading comments, let me be clear—I am not. I do not believe lying is right or acceptable. I am simply suggesting that just because you *think* it's true doesn't make it true. Just because you *think* it is so doesn't make it so. I know, I know...this is probably shocking news for some people!

I once went on a blind date (against my better judgment). We had sent each other pictures in advance. At the conclusion of the date, she asked me if I thought she looked like her picture. I said, "You know, a photo captures a person at only one moment in time; you don't get a real picture until you meet her." She said, "You know, when I got your picture, I thought you were really good-looking, but now that I have met you, you are pretty old, tired, and worn out." I asked her why she would say that and she said, "I am just being honest."

Apparently this woman never heard the adage "If you can't say something nice, don't say anything at all!" Why would she (or anyone else) think that just because something may be true it ought to be communicated? There are many things that are *definitely* true that should never be communicated!

Here are the filters for what and how you should communicate the truth:

1. Ask yourself: Is what I am about to say factually accurate?

2. Ask yourself: Is what I am about to say useful for the listener?

3. Ask yourself: Is what I am about to say constructive for the listener?

4. If you decide you must share your opinion, make sure to let the listener know that it is just that, an opinion.

5. Be as open to his feedback as you expect him to be to yours.

CHAPTER
FORTY-ONE

L I F E ☑ L E S S O N

Is Your Life About Transition or Transformation?

You and I experience about 20,000 moments a day. Negative, positive, or neutral, they are moments nonetheless. Many of those moments result in change—change in thought, change of plans, change of attitude, and so forth. My question for you is this: Are the changes that happen in your life and work simply transitions or are they about transformation? Do you transition from one thing to another in a "reactive" or "adaptive" way, or are you being intentional in the way you deal with change?

If you were changing positions in your organization, *transitional* thinking would be about the money, status, and prestige. *Transformational* thinking/living would be about how it will affect who you are, its effect on your values and way of life. I want to encourage you to live and work in a state of transformation.

Transformation involves revolution or alteration. It is about creating a new way of being, not just doing things differently.

Here are some keys to transformational living:

1. Think through the changes in your life before you make them.

2. Ask yourself questions like: *How will this change affect me, those I work with, and those I care about? What can I do to ensure positive personal transformation?*

3. Consider the unintended consequences of these changes.

4. Ask yourself: *How will I be different as a result of this change?*

5. If it is a change that is happening to you, how will you internalize it in such a way that it positively affects you at a deep level?

6. Be intentional about how you deal with the changes in your life.

CHAPTER
FORTY-TWO

LIFE ✓ LESSON

Is Your Life Balanced?

If it is, stop reading this and begin to write your own book. You will most likely get very wealthy!

I didn't ask if you knew something about balance or if you attended a seminar on the subject or if you are "working on" becoming more balanced. I mean, is your life *really balanced*? I hope not. I think life balance is a futile pursuit, and it leads to unnecessary pressure and guilt.

Let's get this straight: My life is not balanced. Whew, I feel so much better now!

Perhaps you're beating yourself up over the fact that your career takes you away from your kids. Well, there's some very interesting research about what kids want from their parents. Very few kids want more time. What most kids want is for their parents to be happy when they do spend time with them. So consider this chapter your "get-out-of-life-balance-free" card.

Stop pushing so hard and take a minute to breathe. Life presents opportunities every day. We choose to engage or disengage based on how those activities align with what we value. Overall, do you make choices to engage in life at a level that energizes and fulfills you, or is it about the relentless pursuit of _____ (you fill in the blank)? I am counseling you to look at life like a buffet. You get to make choices in the five key areas of life (not every area, every day, though).

Here are those areas with examples:

1. **Recreational**—A choice to play

   - When do you play?

   - How do you relax?

2. **Physical**—A choice to take care of your body on all levels

   - Some days it's French fries; some days it's carrots.

   - Does your heart rate ever change? (You don't have to run a marathon, but you do need *some* exercise!)

3. **Emotional**—A choice to build emotionally enriching experiences

   - Are your personal relationships, such as romantic relationships and friendships, fun and fulfilling?

   - Are you truly engaged when you spend time with family?

4. **Spiritual**—A choice to be connected to something bigger than you

   - Acts of service.

   - Being in a place of gratitude.

5. **Intellectual**—A choice to be in a space of learning

   - Challenge yourself by asking questions.

   - When was the last time you were interested enough to explore?

The key is quality, not quantity. Being mindful and fully engaged in every choice you make, in every area of life, is far preferable to striving for some artificial goal like "balance." So let it go...and enjoy your life!

CHAPTER
FORTY-THREE

L I F E ✓ L E S S O N

Are Commitments "Head" Things or "Heart" Things?

When I speak, I often ask that question. Most of the time people say commitments (at least real ones) come from the heart. I don't want to take the romance out of it or anything, but I disagree. Commitments, at least real ones, *always* come from the head first.

Have you ever made an expensive impulse purchase or, I don't know, married someone in Vegas you met the night before? Obviously, that was an emotional/heart decision. As you probably discovered, making a decision at a moment of high emotional intensity is usually a bad idea. No financial obligation or relationship should ever be entered into without first considering your willingness and ability to commit. The "considering" takes place in the head, not the heart.

Here is the Mike Staver definition of commitment: "Making a decision or choice about a specific result." The key to commitment is understanding it's a *decision*, a choice. Anyone who knows me knows that I put a huge emphasis on taking responsibility for your choices. Commitments are always reflected in behavior. If I say I will meet you at 6:00 for dinner and I don't show up, clearly I was *not* committed (accident not withstanding).

Here are the steps to ensuring your commitments are "head" things first:

1. Carefully consider what you commit to.

2. Focus on aligning your commitments with your behavior.

3. Act regardless of how you feel. If you allow emotion to drive your decisions, you will find yourself undependable or erratic in your behavior.

4. Remain flexible. You are allowed to change your mind.

5. Keep in mind that the more serious the commitment, the more damage will be done if you break it.

Look, we are here for only a short time. Our commitments—to partners, children, work, friends—are important because when we string them all together, they make up the very fabric of our lives. Do not enter into them lightly. Start with your head, then continue with your heart.

CHAPTER
FORTY-FOUR

L I F E ☑ L E S S O N

Could You Work at Nordstrom?

In most organizations, there are policies on top of policies. They enforce endless orientation training to be certain that everyone understands the rules around customer service and how to treat people. More money was spent last year on customer service training than on any other topic besides leadership development training. And yet, I can't help but notice that customer service just gets worse and worse. How is it possible that a company can spend tens (or hundreds) of thousands of dollars on service programs and training, and yet, customers *still* are not treated well?

Perhaps all the rules and programs and training are, themselves, the problem. Maybe taking all discretion out of the hands of employees and trying to legislate every word they say is a mistake. Nordstrom seems to think so. The upscale department store chain has thrown out conventional "wisdom" and has only one rule in its handbook: "Always use your best judgment." Can it really be that simple? Does it really boil down to using good judgment? Based on Nordstrom's success, I would say yes, it does.

So to what extent does this principle apply to you in every area of your life? Do you stop long enough to think through your judgment? I am convinced that in our hectic lives, driven by the breakneck pace we're expected to keep up, we overcomplicate the keys to success. To what extent are you committed to pausing long enough to always use your best judgment? How would your life change if you always practiced that pause?

Right now, you might be saying, "Hey, Mike, I always use my best judgment!" Let me respectfully suggest you are in denial. Nobody *always* uses his or her best judgment, but I think it is a worthy goal. What would it take for you to use your best judgment every hour of every day? What kind of discipline would it require? If you are actually considering those questions, then I suggest you are using good judgment already.

Here are some ways to ensure you are using good judgment:

1. Stop and think about what you are about to do and what is the right thing to do in this situation.

(Okay, I guess it was only one way!)

That's it! Now go start exercising good judgment!

CHAPTER
FORTY-FIVE

Did You Know That Perception Is Not Reality?

There are many empty phrases out there that people routinely (and thoughtlessly) use. "Perception is reality" is one of them. It is a wise person who listens intently to the flippant things people sometimes say to see if they *really* hold water. Someone once uttered this (now trite) phrase, and a group of people thought *Oooohhhhhhh, that is so true!* But the truth is, it is *not* true. If perception were reality, then I would perceive that I look like Matthew McConaughey and—poof!—it would be real. I assure you, I do not look even remotely like Matthew.

It is true that perception tends to be more powerful than reality when that perception is accepted as truth. The profoundly thin woman who perceives that she is fat continues on a destructive course of dieting. The guy who thinks he never measures up tends to overcompensate for his "shortcomings." The kid who believes he

103

never gets attention acts out. If perception were reality, there would be no such thing as magic. (Hellooooo, that's why they call it magic, because it plays with our perceptions!) Still, just because you perceive something does not make it so.

I was in a meeting the other day with a client and someone said, "The customer didn't think we did a good job, so since perception is reality, we didn't do a good job!" WHAT?! It is critical, in this case, that the client acknowledge the customer's perception and do what they can to make it right. But it would be more authentic to say, "When perception and reality are in conflict, reality usually loses."

Here are some ways to be certain you are dialed into reality:

1. Make a rigorous examination of the facts.

2. Acknowledge the discrepancy between perception and reality.

3. If it is your perception/reality conflict, act only on what is real—not what you *think* is real.

4. If someone else is experiencing the perception/reality conflict, acknowledge her perception and work to solve the problem she perceives. If an employee perceives that he is getting treated differently from others, then ask a question like, "What would need to happen to change this perception?"

CHAPTER
FORTY-SIX

L I F E ☑ L E S S O N

Have You Mastered the Three Skills Everyone Should Have?

There are really only three things you have to know in order to be successful. You've probably learned these things already and forgotten them due to being distracted by all the other garbage that you have been told you need to know. Every kid in every high school in America wonders why he has to learn some of the stuff he does, and guess what? Many teachers wonder the same thing. Don't let what really matters get lost in a vortex of useless trivia.

I hope you're not struggling to search for the magic lamp being held by the ancient wizard who will unlock all of life's secrets for you. It's not that complicated. If you will focus on three things about to be revealed, I guarantee that you will be more successful, more fulfilled, more energized, and less annoying to the people around you. You have finally found the only three things you really ever need to know. *Everything* you will *ever* need to do or be is here. Master these things and you'll never need to worry about anything else.

Here are the three skills you need to have:

1. You need to know how to solve problems independently.

   Problems will present themselves constantly. Call them opportunities or call them apples, but just don't call them lemons. (I hate clichés!) Whatever you call your problems, they aren't fun and they probably aren't going to solve themselves. And if you are waiting to have problems solved for you, you will be waiting in line a long time. Go to a class, read a book, or just practice solving problems independently. It doesn't matter if you mess things up; just work to solve problems without relying on someone else. Oh, and while you're at it, do the world a favor and *stop* solving other people's problems. Lend counsel, expertise, and encouragement, but *don't* fix the problem for someone else unless it's life-threatening and he genuinely can't fix it himself.

2. You need to know how to communicate effectively.

   Of all the things you need to know how to do, you must be able to communicate. Not talk, communicate. Here are three things to do in order of importance:

   i. Explore—Basically, this means asking good questions.

   ii. Acknowledge the other person's perceptions as real to her.

   iii. Respond non-judgmentally to what you learn.

3. You need to know how to play well with others.

   Last, but not least, learn how to build constructive, healthy relationships. The mark of a successful person is how effectively he gets along with others despite differences. (By the way, this doesn't mean you have to like everyone.) How do you know if you play well with others? Listen to how much fault you find in other people and that will be a good measure. If you find more fault than right, you need to work on this.

CHAPTER
FORTY-SEVEN

Do You Stand Out?
(In a Good Way?)

If you don't stand out, you need to read this *very* carefully. If you stand out for reasons you'd rather not stand out for, then you need to read carefully, quickly, and twice!

Regardless of the size of the organization you work in or the position you hold, it is best if you stand out. That doesn't mean you have to be loud or attention-seeking. It *does* mean that in any enterprise, people who are outstanding tend to make more, know more, and be thought of more highly. They tend not to get lost. Most of the time, you stand to gain more by standing out.

The challenge is balancing the "stand out" side of the paradox with the "humility" side of it. Have you ever known a person who is immensely talented and yet doesn't seem to get the opportunities? I am certain there are multiple factors involved, but for the purposes of this chapter, let's look at the things that will ensure that you stand out anywhere in your life *and* that you remain humble and in alignment with your values.

Here are five ways to stand out (in a good way):

1. Be focused on solutions, not problems. Find ways to solve problems or at least be in a mindset that is solution-oriented. No boss or colleague or life partner wants to hear about problems all the time, especially if those problems are left unsolved.

2. Be clear about your role and responsibilities. Exceed those expectations. If you are hired to sell roses, don't spend your time rearranging the flower shop (even if it needs rearranging) unless and until every rose is sold.

3. Be enthusiastic.

4. Create energy by staying flexible and driven.

5. Be hungry to learn and develop all the time, every day. The best way to do this is through rigorous self-evaluation. Pointing fingers is annoying and will drop you to the bottom of the sea of mediocrity quickly.

CHAPTER
FORTY-EIGHT

L I F E ☑ L E S S O N

Do You Work Hard?

The world is full of people who want you to think that hard work will get you what you want. We tell kids to work hard and they will be successful. Even in this book, I have encouraged you to "do the work." I am not suggesting that hard work is bad. I am suggesting that hard work is never enough. I am stating that hard work alone has little, if any, chance of getting you where you need to be in the way you need to get there. There are those who say, "No, you shouldn't work harder; you should work smarter." Are you kidding me? Anyone who says this has either just been to some seminar and can't think of anything more intelligent to say or she thinks you have been working dumber for all of recent memory!

Don't misunderstand, it is important to work hard as long as that hard work has certain characteristics associated with it. You can work really hard at something that doesn't matter and find yourself completely exhausted with little to show for it. On the other hand, you can achieve significant results without a sense of character and values and be left with empty accomplishment. What is the emphasis in your life and the lives of those you influence? Do you have a consistent balance between character and competence? To what extent are you willing to allow your life to be a model of these two critical characteristics? Do you have regular conversations with those you influence about the critical balance between character and competence? Don't assume people know! Don't think for one second that those you influence and care about just naturally "get it." They don't. It is critical to not only model but to talk about and provide resources for the development of character and competence.

How to develop character:

1. Identify the character qualities you most want to have.
2. Identify the behaviors that go with those qualities.
3. Practice the behaviors even if they feel uncomfortable.
4. Tolerate imperfection.

How to develop competence:

1. Be in a mindset of learning.
2. Learn.
3. Apply what you learn.
4. Accept failure as a necessary part of gaining competence.
5. Develop new ways to apply what you learn every time you fail.

CHAPTER
FORTY-NINE

L I F E ☑ L E S S O N

Is It True That Change Is Really That Difficult?

So it's true that change is inevitable. It's true that nothing happens until something changes. It's true that change is what drives personal and professional growth. All of that sounds great, right? But if change is "all that" then why do some people thrive in the midst of change while others struggle? Why do some people collapse under the weight of uncertainty while others strap themselves in for the ride? There has to be another explanation other than their personality...or lack of it.

It occurred to me this week that after all the clichés are spoken and all the easy answers are tried, it boils down to three critical elements in dealing with whatever change presents itself. Before I go into them, let me say this: All change is either self-initiated (a job change, a move, beginning an exercise program), or imposed on us by outside forces (a layoff, the death of a significant person in your life, a change in health, winning the lottery). Either way, change is challenging. (Yes, even winning the lottery.) You can't deal with change with enthusiasm alone.

Here are the three things you need in order to handle change (good or bad) effectively:

1. Relationships—What are the relationships that you have that would support you during the transition? Who in your life will tell you the truth and stand with you even if one of their feet is kicking your butt? If you don't have such relationships, please, strive to develop them. Get connected in your company, your community, and so on.

2. Resources—What are the resources available to you? Resources include people, finances, attitude, and so forth. Leveraging all available resources is key to working through change effectively. Whenever you are in a moment of emotional intensity, your brain considers only what it takes to protect you. This often means it ignores resources that may be very useful to you. Consider who or what might make the transition smoother and more productive.

3. Relentlessness—Navigating change requires you to persevere, sometimes against a significant current. Stop expecting it to be easy. Stop wishing it felt better and press on. *Yeah, yeah, yeah,* I know it's hard! Press on anyway! Most people who navigate change well are schooled in the art of sticking with it.

CHAPTER
FIFTY

L I F E ☑ L E S S O N

Is It Knowledge or Understanding?

Okay, you know...but do you understand? You know what she said, but do you understand what she meant? You know your kid is having trouble getting along with you, but do you understand why and how to fix it? You know smoking is bad for you, but do you understand the impact on your health? You know there is a lot of talk about global warming, but do you understand enough about it to form an intelligent opinion? You know...but do you really understand?

The fundamental difference between knowing and understanding has to do with what you do with what you know. It's about being conscious in your choices and living and acting on purpose. It's about parking all of the rationalizations and spin so that you really and completely *understand*. Understanding has to do with recognizing, comprehending, identifying with, or grasping. At the core of it, it's really about how willing you are to stop and pay attention long enough to get what something really means and how you can influence it. Most of the time, we are so busy processing information that we take little time to understand what it means on a personal, as well as more general, scale.

Here's how to move yourself to a life that's more about understanding:

1. *Stop* and pay attention to the information you are receiving.

2. Ask insightful questions until you understand, *really* understand.

3. Realize that sometimes caring enough to really understand may be enough.

4. Determine to what extent you need to do something with what you understand. If she doesn't think you care and you really understand, then perhaps you should do something with that information. If your son is struggling in his relationship with you, perhaps you should do something with that.

5. Evaluate the outcome of those things you did or didn't do and determine what adjustments to your behavior you need to make.

CHAPTER
FIFTY-ONE

L I F E ☑ L E S S O N

The Problem with Hope

I have found that one of the biggest dangers people face when they are working through life's inevitable ups and downs sounds harmless. In fact, it sounds downright positive. *Hope.* We hope things will get better; we hope that sale will come in; we hope the relationship will improve; we hope we'll be able to find a job. Here is the problem...hope doesn't get it done. All of us have at least one area of our lives where hope is bigger than our actions.

Hope alone will not and cannot create desirable outcomes for us. In fact, if we are not careful, it will cause us to recoil from what needs to get done.

In many cases hope can be as paralyzing as hopelessness. Hope always feels better—and I believe we should have it—but it is never enough. Hope alone will leave you feeling better and accomplishing little. I realize that this can seem somewhat paradoxical, and that some people will feel uncomfortable with the idea. Still, I encourage you to consider areas of your life in which you are letting hope take the place of action. I was watching the news just now, and they were talking about a cruise ship in the Antarctic that hit an iceberg and began to sink. When the spokesperson for the cruise line was being asked questions about their procedures, ironically, he never said, "Well, first of all, we kept hoping that the hole wasn't really there."

Here are some ways to ensure that what you're hoping will happen actually will:

1. Identify any area of your life where hope is bigger than action (all of us have at least one).

2. Determine what needs to be done and immediately do something.

3. Be *persistent* in activities that will ensure that your hope is not in vain.

4. Surround yourself with people who will encourage hope while holding you accountable for action.

5. Stop believing that hope is enough. Simply, it isn't.

CHAPTER
FIFTY-TWO

What Is Your Dream?

It happened during a break in the morning session of a seminar I was doing in Cincinnati, Ohio. The topic was "How to Stay Calm and Productive Under Pressure." I had completed the morning session by asking the age-old question *If you could do anything with your life—I mean anything—and you were guaranteed success, what would you do?* When I ask that question to groups, most people resist answering, saying the question is not realistic. At this point I reply, "So what? I still want an answer." A man walked up to me at the break and said he wanted to be a chef. He said he had always wanted to be a chef, and his dream had never changed. I asked him what he was doing now, and he told me he was an engineer and that he came from a long line of engineers.

I suspect this man has lots of company. The research is clear that most people, if given the opportunity, would be doing something other than what they currently do. Whether that is true for you or not, I am certain that there is a dormant dream in you somewhere. If you have read this far in my book, you know I am not a pie-in-the-sky idealist. Sometimes, in fact, I may be too harsh in my relentless pursuit of reality. Still, I believe in dreams. Let me be clear: You were born to dream and to pursue your dream. Do not delay in reawakening that dream. Do not come to the end of your life without every last drop of possibility drained from your tanks.

Johnny Depp was once asked, "When you die and get to the Other Side, what do you hope God says first?" Johnny Depp replied, "I hope He says, 'WOW!'" I *love* that! If you determine that you will let your dreams die—and I hope you will not—then do the world this favor: If you have kids, insist that they dream and live in a state of wonder. Encourage them, even force them, to talk about their dreams and to pursue them with every ounce of energy they have. *Never* discourage them! You don't have a clue what your kids are truly capable of.

And this doesn't apply only to your kids. Do not continually tell the people around you that something isn't realistic. No invention, cure for disease, engineering marvel, major athletic accomplishment, or world-changing event was *ever* realistic at the time it occurred! So don't be the Eeyore in anyone's life. Encourage and uplift people in pursuit of their passion. They will like you more, and you will feel better. But the greatest hope I have is that it will reawaken you.

Here is how to live a dream:

1. Identify your dream. Do not be shy. Let it all out.

2. Determine how big it is.

3. Surround yourself with people who encourage and support the dream. Do not share it with those who will discourage you. If you do make this mistake and she turns out to be a downer, tell her to shut up and go away.

4. Immediately begin to take steps toward your dream. Momentum happens when behaviors are executed in sequence quickly.

5. Celebrate every small win.

Pursuing your dreams adds richness and color to your life. In fact, a life *not* fueled by dreams is barely a life at all. It's merely an existence. So...decide to become that chef or pilot or writer or photojournalist or racecar driver, starting today. Go ahead: Make God say WOW!

That's all. I'll shut up now.

MORE ABOUT MIKE

Mike Staver is CEO of The Staver Group, a national team of strategic advisors and coaches who help people and organizations get from where they are to where they want to be.

Get more of Mike!

Book him to speak at your next event.
Work with him or one of his coaches one-on-one.
Purchase more of his products.

Contact Mike at:

Web site: www.TheStaverGroup.com
E-mail: info@TheStaverGroup.com
Phone: 904-321-0877

OTHER RESOURCES BY MIKE

Multiple CD Package:
21 Ways to Defuse Anger and Calm People Down

CDs or Mp3 Downloads:
Achieving Success
Communicating with the Opposite Sex
Defusing Anger in Others
Fundamentals of Leadership
How to Identify and Correct Employee Performance Problems
Outstanding Communication
Resolving Conflict
Staying Calm Under Pressure

Books:
Motivational Leaders

To purchase, please visit www.TheStaverGroup.com.

NOTES

NOTES